CAT

THE DARK END OF THE STREET

WOMAN

CATW

THE DARK END OF THE STREET

ED **BRUBAKER** WRITER DARWYN **COOKE** MIKE **ALLRED** CAMERON **STEWART** ARTISTS

MATT **HOLLINGSWORTH** COLORIST SEAN **KONOT** LETTERER

CATWOMAN: THE DARK END OF THE STREET

Published by DC Comics.

Originally published in single magazine form in
DETECTIVE COMICS 759-762, CATWOMAN 1-4.

DC Comics, 1700 Broadway,
New York, NY 10019
A Warner Bros. Entertainment Company
Printed in Canada. Third Printing.
ISBN: 1-56389-908-6
ISBN 13: 978-1-56389-908-9
Cover illustration by Darwyn Cooke.

CATWOMAN: THE DARK END OF THE STREET

I'm back in Gotham for two weeks, and it already feels like I'm home again...

Now I'm starting to remember the screwed-up parts of this city instead of just thinking about all those great restaurants in Chinatown.

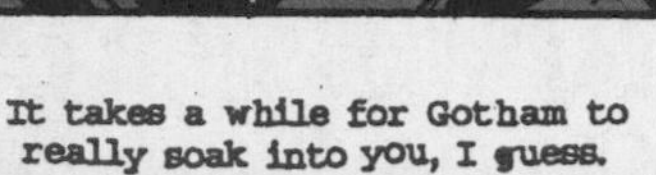

It takes a while for Gotham to really soak into you, I guess.

Like the class division. The harsh split between the Haves and Have-Nots that has, if anything, gotten worse in recent times.

Then of course, there's the Batman. Gotham's own vigilante hero, who for some reason likes to pretend he's a myth.

In the old days, it was nice to think he might not be real...

... but I know better now.

And, going hand in hand with that freak of the night, is the incredible amount of corruption in the city.
SLAM BRADLEY
TRAIL of the CATWOMAN
PART 1
From the street-level cops, all the way to the politicians. It's as dirty as any town I've ever seen.
Which is kind of a funny observation, considering where I am today...
NOW THEN, DID MY SECRETARY GIVE YOU ANY INFORMATION ABOUT WHY I WANTED TO SEE YOU?
SHE SAID IT WAS A MISSING PERSONS CASE.
IT IS, IT IS... AND KIND OF A COMPLICATED ONE.
BUT I WAS TOLD YOU WERE ESPECIALLY GOOD AT FINDING PEOPLE.
I'M GOOD AT A COUPLE THINGS, THAT'S JUST ONE OF THEM. WHO IS IT THAT'S MISSING, AND WHY NOT JUST HAVE THE COPS LOOK FOR THEM?
AS I RECALL, THE MAYOR HAS A PRETTY DECENT SIZE POLICE FORCE AT HIS DISPOSAL.
WRITTEN BY
ED BRUBAKER
ARTWORK BY
DARWYN COOKE & CAMERON STEWART
LETTERING BY
SEAN KONOT
COLOR & SEPARATIONS BY
MATT HOLLINGSWORTH
EDITED BY
MATT IDELSON

WELL, THAT'S *PART* OF WHY IT'S COMPLICATED.
SEE, I WANT TO KEEP THIS *LOW PROFILE*, AND AS FAR AS THE *POLICE BRASS* IN THIS CITY ARE CONCERNED, THE PERSON I WANT YOU TO FIND IS *DEAD*.

THAT *DOES* COMPLICATE THINGS, BUT I CAN *PROBABLY* FIND A TOMBSTONE IF YOU WANT ME TO.

YOU MISUNDERSTAND, MR. BRADLEY. SHE IS *NOT* DEAD... AT LEAST, I *REFUSE* TO BELIEVE SHE IS UNTIL I SEE A *CORPSE*.
SHE?
CATWOMAN. MAYBE YOU'VE HEARD OF HER?

SURE. A MASKED *CAT BURGLAR* SUPPOSED TO BE ONE OF THE *BEST*.
WHEN WAS SHE SUPPOSED TO HAVE DIED?

A FEW WEEKS AGO... BUT AS I SAID, I *DON'T* BELIEVE IT. I THINK SHE'S GONE INTO *HIDING*, AND I WANT *YOU* TO FIND HER.
CAN YOU DO IT?

FINDING SOMEONE WITHOUT A *NAME* IS GONNA BE PRETTY *TOUGH*, MR. MAYOR. ESPECIALLY IF THEY MIGHT *ACTUALLY* BE DEAD... BUT I CAN CERTAINLY GIVE IT A *SHOT*.
WHAT HAVE YOU GOT ON HER?
NOT MUCH... WHAT WE *DID* HAVE WAS DESTROYED OR *STOLEN*. SHE DOESN'T *LIKE* PEOPLE KEEPING TABS ON HER.

MY SECRETARY WILL GIVE YOU HER FILE.
ALL RIGHT, THEN I'LL GET RIGHT TO WORK... OH, *ONE THING, MR. MAYOR*...
... WHY DO YOU WANT HER *FOUND* SO BADLY?

THAT'S MY *PERSONAL* CONCERN, MR. BRADLEY. JUST DO YOUR JOB AND LET *ME* WORRY ABOUT THAT.

AND REMEMBER, THIS INVESTIGATION IS *CONFIDENTIAL*.

So the Mayor of Gotham wants me to find a cat burglar that his own police think is deceased, and he wants me to keep a lid on it.

I could tell I'd have to find my own leads on this one, though the police report did give me a few ideas.

She was a thorn in the side of a lot of the old crime bosses, as I recall. Stole from the crooked politicians and the borough chiefs.

And at some point, she moved from preying on the guilty to just stealing from anyone who had something worth stealing.

... or in her case, I guess, Cat and Bat.

KLANG!

But in there somewhere...

... between the girl who took on the mob...

My first idea was to check with a fence on the East End who, a few years ago, had gotten caught with some diamonds that got traced back to Catwoman.

As it happens, I had a prior acquaintance with the fence in question, Leonard "Swifty" Burgess.

He even buzzed some of his friends to see if they could be of any assistance.

Unfortunately, they didn't have a lot to offer.

CRUNCH

NOT TOO SHABBY FOR AN OLD GUY...

...EVEN IF I DO SAY SO MY--

WHAM!

URRK--!

AAAGH!

SKKAAASH

NOW, DO YOU WANNA ANSWER MY QUESTIONS, OR DO I HAVE'TA COME OVER THE COUNTER, TOO?
PAWNSHOP

WHA... WHADDAYA WANNA KN-KNOW?

CATWOMAN. WHAT DO YOU KNOW ABOUT HER? AND DON'T BOTHER LYIN', 'CAUSE I KNOW YOU WERE FENCIN' STUFF FOR HER.

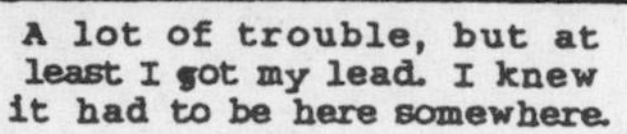
A lot of trouble, but at least I got my lead. I knew it had to be here somewhere.

SLAM BRADLEY
'TRAIL' of the 'CATWOMAN'
'PART 2'
Private eyes have a bad rap as creeps who'll dig up any kind of dirt for a paycheck.
And it's true, some will gleefully ruin people and dance all the way to the bank.
I'm not that kind of guy, though. I hate digging into people's pasts, because usually what you find is just a disappointment. Mistakes, insecurities, greed...
But as much as I hate it, sometimes you need to find out what's buried to get at the truth.
SELINA KYLE
Like tonight, for example, I had to do some fairly unpleasant digging.
But Selina Kyle was the only real lead I had in this case, and you don't let go of a lead until you're absolutely certain it's a dead end.
WRITTEN BY ED BRUBAKER
ARTWORK BY DARWYN COOKE
LETTERING BY SEAN KONOT
COLOR & SEPARATIONS BY MATT HOLLINGSWORTH
EDITED BY MATT IDELSON
CORONER

the Thin Blue line
But who knew yesterday I'd be exhuming corpses just to eliminate doubt?
I was just following the tip I had gotten from Swifty, and interviewing one of the investigating officers in Catwoman's prison break.

THE MAYOR TOLD ME TO COOPERATE, BRADLEY... BUT I DON'T KNOW WHAT YOU WANT ME TO SAY...
I'M INTERESTED IN WHAT ANGLE YOU AND YOUR PARTNER WERE PURSUING...

ANGLE? WASN'T MANY TO CHOOSE FROM... WE GOT A WOMAN WHO'S NOT IN THE SYSTEM ANYWHERE.
HAVE IS SHE LOOKS A LOT LIKE A LADY WHO WAS RECENTLY KILLED WHILE RUNNING FOR MAYOR OF NEW YORK.

SELINA KYLE, RIGHT? I HEARD THE COPS HAD CATWOMAN UNDER THE MICROSCOPE ON THAT ONE, TOO.
YEAH, BUT THAT WAS N.Y.P.D., NOT GOTHAM. STILL, WE FOLLOW THIS KYLE CONNECTION AS FAR AS IT LEADS...

... AND WE COME UP WITH MAGGIE KYLE. YOUNGER SISTER OF THE DECEASED...
... THING IS, WE CAN'T TRACK HER DOWN.

HEARD SHE JOINED A CONVENT OR SOMETHIN' TEN YEARS AGO...

AND FROM THERE IT WAS JUST BUBKISS. THEN CATWOMAN GETS KILLED, SO WHO CARES?
I GUESS YOUR MAYOR DOES, FOR ONE.

WHATEVER. MY OPINION, HE'S WASTING YOUR TIME AND HIS MONEY.
WELL, LUCKILY, THERE'S PLENTY OF BOTH TO GO AROUND...

... THANKS FOR THE COOPERATION, DETECTIVE.

And how do I go from there to a New York graveyard in the middle of the night?

It's simple, really...

I had the Mayor request a copy of the coroner's report on Selina Kyle from New York City, and it turns out there isn't one.

After that it wasn't too hard for him to pull a few strings and have her dug up on the Q.T.

And I do keep it in mind, but I can't just sit around and twiddle my thumbs waiting for the phone to ring. So the next afternoon, I go to visit a reporter I know.

So, between the coroner's report, which I'd probably get later, and the file from Spender, I had enough to keep me busy.

As I pondered all of this, I got a surprise that told me my instincts were right on the money.

Then the elevator just kept falling until gravity had no meaning, and everything was good and right with the world except that my name kept ringing in my ears, like an alarm clock.
Mr Bradley?
Mr Bradley?
Mr Bradley!
PLEASE, MR. BRADLEY... I REALLY *MUST* INSIST WE TALK.

SURE... WHY NOT...?

SO... WHAT CAN I DO FOR YOU, IF YOU DON'T MIND MY ASKING?
IT'S SIMPLE, REALLY...

... MY EMPLOYER HAS BEEN LED TO UNDERSTAND THAT YOU ARE INVESTIGATING THE DEATH OF SELINA KYLE. CORRECT?

I'M AFRAID I'M NOT AT LIBERTY TO SAY.
GINO HAS A GUN TO YOUR HEAD, MR. BRADLEY, AND YOU STILL AREN'T AT LIBERTY TO SAY?

BASICALLY.
OKAY, WE'LL LET IT GO FOR NOW. MY EMPLOYER IS INTERESTED IN HEARING WHAT YOUR INVESTIGATION UNCOVERS, AND HE'S WILLING TO PAY QUITE HANDSOMELY.

I ALREADY HAVE A CLIENT.
LET ME EXPLAIN SOMETHING. MY EMPLOYER PAID CATWOMAN A LARGE SUM FOR THE DEATH OF MS. KYLE, AND WE ARE NOT ENTIRELY SURE THAT IT WAS MONEY WELL SPENT.
WHAT DO YOU MEAN?

WE HAVE OUR DOUBTS THAT ANYONE WAS ACTUALLY KILLED AT ALL. CATWOMAN WASN'T WHAT YOU'D CALL TRUSTWORTHY.
WE SUSPECT THEY MAY HAVE BEEN WORKING TOGETHER, AND WE DON'T APPRECIATE BEING THE VICTIMS OF A CON.
IF YOUR INVESTIGATION SHOULD TURN UP ANYTHING THAT COULD PROVE OUR SUSPICIONS, WE'D BE VERY PLEASED.
I ALREADY SAID--
YOU CAN GO NOW. WE'LL BE IN TOUCH...
NICE HAT, JERK!
DAMMIT!
OWWW!
WHACK!
NO DUMPING

OW.
Later that night, after a hot bath, I'd find it encouraging to know that the mob thought there was a connection, too.
But right now, I was just thinking of how Gino's face would look after I got through with him.

I had to give credit to Spender. His people did good work, and he was right about Selina Kyle. She did have guts and class, which was even rarer after what she'd gone through growing up.

She and her little sister had been knocked around from orphanages to foster homes since she was about ten years old.

They told him of a shy girl who became tough over the years, and who was especially protective of her sister, Maggie.

Then she and Maggie ran away when she was fifteen, and she dropped off the face of the earth, only to resurface six years later in Gotham's high society.

Reading with an eye on the Catwoman connection, it's so obvious. Young Selina Kyle, out on the streets surviving by her wits, and Catwoman's early days of stealing from the local mobsters.

Then she becomes high society Selina Kyle, just around the same time that Catwoman starts to rob from the rich.

WHO CARES ABOUT THE *WORLD*-- DID THEY FIND ANYTHING?

YEAH... BUT JUST BETWEEN YOU AND ME AND THE LAMPPOST... THE CORPSE'S PRINTS MATCHED A D.O.A. FROM THREE DAYS BEFORE SELINA KYLE WAS KILLED.

SLAM BRADLEY
TRAIL of the CATWOMAN
PART 3
WRITTEN BY
ED BRUBAKER
ARTWORK BY
DARWYN COOKE
LETTERING BY
SEAN KONOT
COLOR & SEPARATIONS BY
MATT HOLLINGSWORTH
EDITED BY
MATT IDELSON
Actual Private Eye work, much like real police work, depends a lot on luck. You exhaust every angle, and just hope that something appears.
I'd had some luck already, because my one lead had turned out to be solid-- there was definitely a connection between Catwoman and Selina Kyle.
In fact, I was pretty sure that they were one and the same. Unfortunately, most of the world thought they were both dead, too.
So it was going to take some serious luck to finish this job, and the way it was looking right now, mine was just about used up.
8

Just that morning I had been in the plush offices of one of Gotham's finest citizens.

I THINK I'LL STICK WITH MY EARLIER THOUGHT AND ASK YOU TO LEAVE. OR I COULD CALL SECURITY, IF YOU'D RATHER--

OH, NOW, C'MON... ALL I'M TRYING TO DO IS FIND SOME FACTS OUT, I DON'T SEE HOW--

I SAID, GOOD DAY, SIR!

I wasn't expecting Wayne to clam up like that, it didn't fit in with the laid-back playboy image I was so used to with him. Maybe he'd been closer to Selina than I thought.

And while my mind was on Wayne, I bumped into a friend.

So now the mob was actually tracking my progress, too. Why didn't they just hire their own detective? Maybe I'd ask Gino when I finished breaking his teeth.
JUST GET THE JOB DONE, BRADLEY, OR THE ONLY THING YOU'LL BE READING IS YOUR OBITUARY...
But I couldn't waste time worrying, I had real work to do-- footwork.
Circling outwards from the area where Catwoman was last seen alive, I flashed the photo to see if I could get a hit.
NAH, NEVER SEEN HER...
... SHE'S HOT, THOUGH, I'LL TELL YOU THAT...
... I'D'VE SEEN HER, I SURE AS HELL'D REMEMBER...
... IT'S HARD TO SAY-- DO YOU HAVE ANY OTHER PICTURES?
... WAIT, DOESN'T SHE HAVE A WEBSITE?
... WOW, SHE'S REALLY BEAUTIFUL...
HEY, Y'KNOW WHAT? I HAVE SEEN HER...
... CAN I KEEP THIS?
SWELL

DO YOU HAVE A PAIR OF SCISSORS I COULD BORROW?

"I GAVE THEM TO HER AND SHE WENT INTO THE BATHROOM.

"I MUST'VE HAD TO HELP SOMEONE OR SOMETHING, 'CAUSE I NEVER SAW HER COME OUT... BUT AFTER ABOUT AN HOUR, I WENT TO CHECK IF SHE WAS OKAY...

"...SHE WAS GONE, BUT THERE WAS HAIR ALL OVER THE PLACE... LIKE SHE JUST HACKED IT ALL OFF OR SOMETHING."

So I found someone who'd actually spotted her, but he's right across the street from the train station.

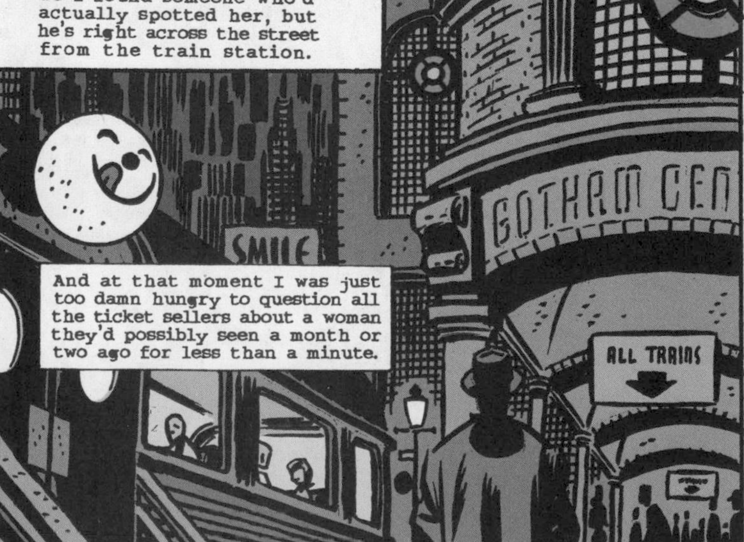

Which would give me time to think about things... One of the dangers of this job.

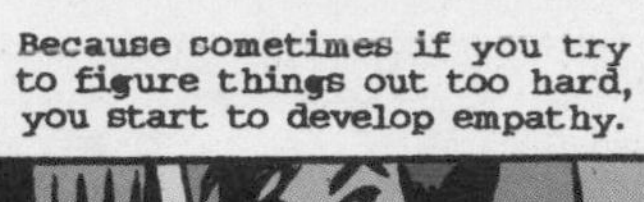

Because sometimes if you try to figure things out too hard, you start to develop empathy.

And then you fill in the blank spots of the story yourself, and start to believe your own fiction.

That's a dangerous line to cross, because one thing a P.I. should know better than just about anybody is that you can never really know anyone.

And yet, there I was, starting to believe I understood this woman the way no one else had.

Understood what she was running from, and that it was something she could never escape, no matter how she might try.

And I was beginning to wonder if I wanted to find her because I was being paid to, or if I just wanted to find her, period.

Right as I'm trying to discern my own motivation, the world goes crazy again.

WE NEED TO TALK.

HEY, LEMME GO!
WHY ARE YOU TRYING TO FIND SELINA KYLE?

ANSWER THE QUESTION!
SHOVE IT! YOU LET ME GO!

OKAY, WE'LL TRY IT YOUR WAY.

AAAGH!

TWANG!
SO...

LET'S TRY THIS AGAIN.

DAMN IT! YOU FREAKIN' NUTJOB! FIRST THE MOB IS IN MY FACE, THEN THE DAMN COPS ARE TELLIN' ME TO KEEP OUT OF IT, AND NOW YOU...

Y'KNOW WHAT?

JUST DROP ME.

OOF!

SELINA KYLE.
SHE'S NOT WHAT YOU THINK...

OH REALLY? YOU MEAN SHE'S NOT CATWOMAN?

I DON'T WANT HER HURT.
REMEMBER THAT, BRADLEY, OR WE'LL MEET AGAIN.
I put on a good tough-guy act, but the second he's gone I'm shaking like a leaf.

What the hell have I gotten myself into? All I want to do is find this girl, and it just turns into more of a mess every day.

I'm beginning to doubt I'll ever find anything but questions, punctuated by an occasional beating.

This job is really starting to seem like more trouble than it's worth, so I guess my next question is why don't I quit?

Which I mull over the entire walk back to my office, failing to come up with a decent answer.

Maybe I was a fool, but for some reason I just felt like I had to see this case through.

I've encountered a lot of bizarre stuff in my years as a P.I. It's a strange line of work, admittedly, and you run into all types.

But in all my days, I've never had the subject of one of my manhunts come looking for me... Until today, that is.

I'M *SELINA KYLE,* MR. BRADLEY, AND I UNDERSTAND YOU'VE BEEN *LOOKING* FOR ME.

CALL ME *SLAM.* "MR. BRADLEY" SOUNDS LIKE SOMEONE'S *TEACHER.*

YOU MIND IF I SMOKE?

NOT AT ALL... YOU'RE PROBABLY WONDERING WHY I'M *HERE,* RIGHT?

IT CROSSED MY MIND.

YEAH, I'LL BET IT DID. WELL, FRANKLY, *SLAM*... YOU'RE A BIT OF A *PROBLEM,* AND WE NEED TO COME TO SOME KIND OF *AGREEMENT.*

HOW AM *I* A PROBLEM?

BECAUSE I *ASKED* ABOUT YOU... AND I HEARD YOU AREN'T THE TYPE OF MAN TO *GIVE UP.*

WRITTEN BY ED BRUBAKER
ARTWORK BY DARWYN COOKE
LETTERING BY SEAN KONOT
COLOR & SEPARATIONS BY MATT HOLLINGSWORTH
EDITED BY MATT IDELSON

SLAM BRADLEY
'TRAIL' of the 'CATWOMAN'
PART 4

WHAT MAKES YOU THINK I COULD'VE *FOUND* YOU, THOUGH?

YOU *COULDN'T* HAVE, BUT YOU'D KEEP SHOWING MY PHOTO AROUND AND ASKING QUESTIONS, AND THEN ALL THE THINGS I WANT TO *BLOW OVER* NEVER WILL...

THAT'S WHY YOU SPLIT? THINGS GOT TOO HOT?

NOT JUST THAT... I CAN HANDLE *HEAT*, BELIEVE ME.

NO, IT'S MORE ABOUT *CONTROL*, I GUESS... SOMETHING MY LIFE SUDDENLY HAD A HUGE *LACK OF*.
IN THE PAST YEAR, THINGS WERE DONE *TO* ME THAT CAUSED MY LIFE TO UNWIND...
AND WHEN I GOT TO THE *BOTTOM* OF IT ALL, I WAS *STILL* LEFT FEELING EMPTY. WHICH MADE ME WONDER HOW MUCH OF IT I HAD CREATED *MYSELF*.

SO I DECIDED IT MIGHT BE BETTER TO JUST *DISAPPEAR* FOR A WHILE.
FORGIVE ME, BUT YOU DON'T EXACTLY SEEM LIKE THE TYPE FOR *SOUL-SEARCHING*, SELINA.

WELL, IT *WAS* A HELL OF A YEAR.

YEAH, SO I GATHERED... BUT WHAT *NOW?* YOU JUST GONNA STAY IN HIDING UNTIL YOU *FIND YOURSELF?*

I'M NOT *SURE* WHAT NOW... SOME OF THAT DEPENDS ON *YOU*, AND WHAT YOU'RE PLANNING TO *DO* WITH THE THINGS YOU'VE PIECED TOGETHER.
KYLE, SELINA

I READ YOUR FILE ON ME, SO I *KNOW* WHAT YOU'VE *GUESSED*.
YEAH, I FIGURED...
WELL, LET ME ASK *YOU* SOMETHING, SELINA...

It's funny, I never admitted it, even to myself, but I think I knew from the first time I read Spender's file on her that I'd never give her up to anyone.

And that was it. She walks in and out, and my whole world is turned upside-down.

It wasn't even what she said, so much as the look in her eyes when she said it. Hopefully that look will get me through whatever hassle the Mayor gives me about quitting.

But right now I don't even care. I'm just listening to her walk away.

Listening to her fade into the distance, knowing I did a good thing.

YOU SHOULD'VE JUST COME TO *ME,* SELINA...

HOW LONG HAVE YOU BEEN FOLLOWING ME?

I WAS FOLLOWING *BRADLEY.* I DIDN'T EXPECT TO SEE YOU.

SO, WHAT DO YOU *WANT?*

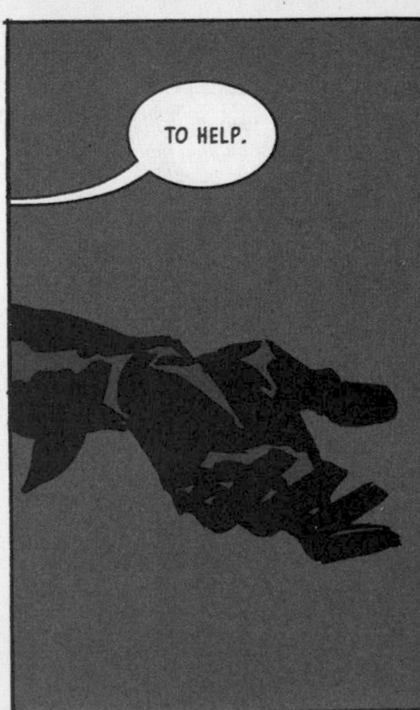
TO HELP.

Not too surprisingly, the Mayor was unhappy about my resignation.

I was thinking for a second that I had gotten off pretty easy.

But they're waiting for me by the time I get to the parking garage.

It's a good beating, to be sure, professional quality.

Like you'd expect from Gotham's Finest.

I put up a bit of a struggle, break a nose, fracture a rib, just so they think I'm trying.

But I know this is my real payment, and the more I fight, the worse it'll be.

So I let them win, I let them through my guard and take it like a man.

And with every blow, I'm seeing Selina's eyes, hearing her voice.

Knowing that every drop of blood is just putting her that much farther out of their reach.

And I hold on to her face like a drunk in a fever dream.

Until they lose interest.
REMEMBER *THIS* NEXT TIME THE MAYOR WANTS SOMETHING, BRADLEY!

And all I can think about, through the pain and the bleeding is...

... It was worth it.

Good thing I burned that file last night, or all this pain would be for nothing. As it is, it looks like I'll be spending a good long while cleaning up and healing up.

But, I've really got nothing better to do today, anyway.

Maybe the day won't be a total wash, after all.

OLD GOTHAM, THE EAST END, FAR TOO LATE...

LOOKIN' FOR A PARTY?
YEAH, I AM, ACTUALLY...

... CAN YOU HELP ME OUT WITH THAT?

OH, I GUESS WE COULD WORK SOMETHIN' OUT...

GET IN.
UNT UH... SORRY, I DON'T DO CAR DATES WITH GUYS I DON'T KNOW.

OKAY, MY NAME'S BRIAN.
GLAD TO MEET YOU...?

I'M LISA.

SEE? NOW WE KNOW EACH OTHER, SO IT'S OKAY, RIGHT?
YEAH, I GUESS SO.

YOU'RE NOT A COP, ARE YOU?

NO... I'M PRETTY SURE I'M NOT A COP.

SMILE

I USUALLY DON'T KISS. BUT MOST OF MY DATES AREN'T AS HANDSOME AS --

HEY, WHAT...
WHAT'S WRONG?! WHAT HAPPENED?

WHAT...?
YOUR FACE... IT'S--

DON'T LOOK AT ME!
I'M NOT--

I JUST--
I SAID--

STOP LOOKING AT ME!

WHAM!!

STOP!
SKGASSH!

LOOKING!
THUMP
THUMP
THUMP

AAAKK*
SMILE

OH, GOD... NO...

I've been having trouble sleeping...

... And my dreams... well, they certainly aren't helping any.

I can't remember much of them-- but I wake up feeling like my whole life is slipping right through my fingers.

anodyne

PART ONE OF FOUR

ED BRUBAKER-WRITER

DARWYN COOKE & MIKE ALLRED-ARTISTS

MATT HOLLINGSWORTH-COLORIST SEAN KONOT-LETTERER

MATT IDELSON-EDITOR NACHIE CASTRO-ASST. EDITOR

AND, FOR SOME REASON, I KEEP THINKING ABOUT MY SISTER...

... BUT I DON'T REALLY KNOW *WHY.*

I MEAN, I HAVEN'T SEEN HER IN... GOD, *YEARS.*

Mmmhmm... WELL, THERE'S NO NEED FOR *MY* PSYCHOANALYSIS.

SOUNDS LIKE YOU'RE DOING A DECENT JOB *YOURSELF,* SELINA...

... YOU'VE GONE THROUGH SOME AWFUL STRUGGLES IN YOUR LIFE. ESPECIALLY IN THIS PAST YEAR...
AND IT'S OBVIOUSLY LEFT SOME SCARS.
HOW LONG HAS IT BEEN NOW SINCE YOU PUT ON THE OUTFIT?

THE OUTFIT? OH, YEAH... THAT.

ALMOST SIX MONTHS.
WELL, YOUR SUBCONSCIOUS IS PROBABLY TRYING TO SORT OUT WHO YOU ARE WITHOUT THAT MASK.
IT DOESN'T TAKE FREUD OR JUNG TO FIGURE THAT OUT.

NO, I GUESS IT DOESN'T. SO ARE YOU TRYING TO TELL ME IT'S NOT DRUGS, IT'S ALL IN MY HEAD?
IN A ROUNDABOUT WAY, YES.

YOUR BLOODWORK CAME BACK CLEAN, SELINA... SEE FOR YOURSELF.
YEAH, hmmm...
I JUST THOUGHT, WITH THIS NOT SLEEPING THING, THAT IT MIGHT STILL BE WORKING ITSELF OUT OF MY SYSTEM.

SORRY TO DISAPPOINT YOU. WHATEVER YOU WERE SUBJECTED TO IS LONG GONE, AS FAR AS I CAN TELL...

... UNLESS YOU WANT ME TO DO A SPINAL TAP?
NO THANKS... I'LL PASS.

SELINA, MY ADVICE, IF YOU REALLY WANT IT, IS TO TAKE ADVANTAGE OF THIS TIME...

... REEVALUATE THINGS, JUST AS YOU'D PLANNED. YOU'VE GIVEN YOURSELF A BREAK FROM YOUR ROUTINE...
... NOW JUST GIVE YOURSELF A BREAK.
THANKS, DR. THOMPKINS. FOR SEEING ME SO LATE...
... AND FOR LISTENING.

CLINIC
IT'S NO TROUBLE, REALLY. WHY ELSE WOULD HE HAVE SENT YOU TO ME?
AND PLEASE, CALL ME LESLIE.
WELL... GOOD NIGHT THEN, LESLIE.

GOT WHAT'CHU NEED...
KIND BUDS... GOT THE KIND BUDS...
RIP
XXX

AIN'T'CHU HEARIN' ME, GIRL? SAID I GOTS WHAT'CHU NEED.

I SINCERELY DOUBT IT.

BWAHAHA!

MAN, GIRL DISSED YOU! AHA!

Welcome home, Selina Kyle...
SMILE

Is this where you belong?
O NOT CROSS
POLICE LINE

But even if it's not, where else were you going to go?
As far as most of the world is concerned, Selina Kyle is dead... So it wasn't like you could just move back into your Park Row apartment.

But this place, no one knows about this place. Not anymore. Well, maybe he knows.
It's hard to say what he knows for sure.

But you hadn't even thought of this place in years. Amazing that it was still here, after all this time, and the changes that Gotham has been through.

But somehow you knew it would be, because you bought this place back in the early days to be a sanctuary...

A safe house for your friends... Holly, Monique, Darla... A secret home away from the street and the life.

Of course, all of them are long gone now, and who would have ever imagined it would be you who would need this sanctuary?

Not to hide, of course... but to slow down, take a look at your life, and the mess you've made of it.
And how fitting that you'd have to come back to these streets, where it all began.
You were a different person then. That Selina took care of people...

... and had been for as long as she could remember...

That had been one of the reasons for the mask, initially. To help provide.
That and the excitement... the adventure. Don't kid yourself that they weren't a big part of it, too.
But when did they take over?

When did you stop helping your sister, your friends, and just start helping yourself?
And when did you climb the social ladder and lose those friends entirely?

SO, THEN... WHO ARE YOU, SELINA KYLE?

Hardly any sleep last night, either.
Maybe what I need is some exercise.

My mind is probably just spinning in circles because I'm not in constant motion.

So, maybe if I work myself to exhaustion, that'll do the trick.
TWAP!

THE GOTHAM GAZETTE
SECOND BODY FOUND IN ONE WEEK
POLICE HAVE NO COMMENT ON MURDER
Anything to just shut my brain off for a few hours.

And if pushing my muscles until they tear doesn't do it...

... maybe, this sunset will...

There's nothing quite like the universe to make your problems feel small...

... if only for a moment or two.

Of course, when night falls there's always something to help you lose perspective...
RATATATTA
ATT

SKREECH

Him. Of course.
BAM!
BRA TA TATTA TAT TAT
Gotham's own guardian angel.

In his black and white world...
KRASH

BOOM

... with his brightly-colored adversaries.
WHEN IS IT TIME... TO ACT LIKE A BANANA...?

WHEN YOU NEED... TO *SPLIT*... HEH HEH HEH...

Such a joke...

Is this my world, too?

With the boy scout...

... and the obsessive-compulsive?
MOVE, DAMN YOU! MOVE!

The violence sure feels like my world.

Without him, I wouldn't have become who I am.

And I owe him so much...

ALL OF YOU! JUST STAY CALM!

NOBODY PANIC, JUST MOVE ONE STEP AT A TIME!

But we've been at odds from the start. Because-- No!

NO!

At odds from the start...

... Because my world is all just shades of grey, Batman.

That's why you'll never really understand me.

It's about good people being forced into bad situations.

That's my territory...

In between right and wrong.

Which is a place you can never go. And we both know it.

Just like I know I'll finally sleep tonight.

mmrrowrr? mrrrowr?

mrrrowr?
WHAT DO YOU WANT, Hmmm? DIDN'T I PUT OUT ENOUGH FOOD, LITTLE FLUFFY GUY?

THEN GO EAT, OKAY? I'VE GOT SOME STUFF TO DO HERE!
mrrraarrr! mrrrrrr!

Dr. Thompkins... Leslie... was right. The mask is part of who I am now.

But it's also part of the problem, too...

... because it became a person all on its own.

So, the question is, how to get rid of that side, all the painful memories and mistakes, take back the mask...
rowrr!

... and still be able to sleep at night. Still be able to live with myself.

I'm not sure if I can do all that, really...

... but I think I know how to try...
SURPLUS
GOV. CODE # 173
PART # H 155 AA

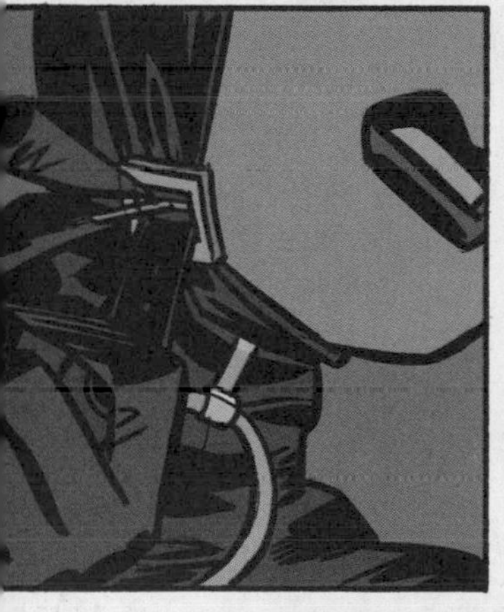

We can skip the tail for now...

And figure out what else to skip as time goes on.

It feels good to be a part of it all again.

The city lights...

The night...

Maybe it feels right again, for the first time in a long time.

SO, WAS THAT *YOU* THE OTHER DAY?

COULDN'T LET HIM *SHOOT* YOU, COULD I?
I'D HAVE SURVIVED IT.

YOU'RE WELCOME.

WHAT IS *THIS*, EXACTLY? THE *NEW YOU*?
I'M NOT *SURE* YET. WHAT DO YOU *THINK*?

IT LOOKS... *PRACTICAL*.
THAT'S WHAT *I* THOUGHT, TOO.

SO, DID YOU GO TO SEE DR. THOMPKINS?
YEAH, A FEW TIMES, ACTUALLY... YOU TOLD HER WHO I *WAS*?

I TRUST HER IMPLICITLY. YOUR SECRET'S *SAFE* WITH HER.
I'M *NOT* MAD.
IT'S KIND OF *NICE*, HAVING SOMEONE KNOW I'M STILL AROUND...

WHAT ARE YOU GOING TO DO? NOW THAT YOU'RE THROUGH WITH YOUR BREAK?
YOU MEAN, WHAT CAN YOU EXPECT FROM ME?
I GUESS WE'LL JUST HAVE TO WAIT AND SEE, WON'T WE?

I GUESS WE WILL.

SO, YOU HAVE TO TELL ME WHY.
WHY WHAT?

WHY DID YOU HELP ME?

WHY, AFTER EVERYTHING THAT I'VE DONE, DID YOU STILL HAVE FAITH IN ME?

I JUST DO, SELINA... NO MATTER WHAT, I BELIEVE THAT DEEP DOWN, YOU'RE REALLY A GOOD PERSON.

DON'T YOU THINK SO?
SOMETIMES... YEAH, SOMETIMES I DO...

... BUT I THINK IT'S JUST A LOT MORE COMPLICATED THAN THAT.

THANK YOU.

Maybe this will actually work.
I'll have to give it time.

But the mask felt good again... It felt like me.

Whoever that is --
CHK
CHK
CLK

CHK
CHK
-- WHAT THE HELL?
CHK

SOMEONE TRYING TO PICK MY LOCK?

CHK
CLK

AHH! WAIT!

OH... MY... GOD...
HOLLY?
SELINA? WHAT ARE YOU DOING HERE?
I THOUGHT--?

YOU'RE BACK ON THE STREETS? OH, HOLLY...
DON'T LOOK AT ME LIKE THAT, SELINA.

YOU DON'T UNDERSTAND...
SO MAKE ME.

THIS'S JUST SO WEIRD... I JUST REMEMBERED WHERE I HID THESE KEYS, BECAUSE I NEEDED SOMEPLACE SAFE TO CRASH.

BUT I NEVER THOUGHT I'D RUN INTO YOU! WE ALL THOUGHT--

WAIT-- WHAT DO YOU MEAN BY SAFE?
WHAT'S WRONG?

BUT, IF YOU'RE BACK...

... YOU MUST KNOW, SELINA...

... SOMEONE'S KILLING US OUT THERE.

LIQUOR
JOE'S

LOOKING FOR A DATE, MISTER?
YOU *READ MY MIND...* GET IN.
LIQUOR

YOU AIN'T *VICE,* ARE YOU?
NO, I'VE *GOT* A FEW THOUGH, WHICH IS WHY I'M LOOKING FOR A *DATE.*

Heh... YEAH, OKAY.

I'M MINDY, CASE YOU NEED TO *CALL ME* SOMETHIN'...

NICE TO MEET YOU, MY NAME'S *GREG.*

HEY, WHAT HAPPENED TO YOUR *WINDOW* BACK HERE?
WHAT...?

Oh, uh... JUST HAD A LITTLE *ACCIDENT...*

LIQUOR
JOE'S
DING!
DING!
DING!
DING!
DING!
DING!
HEADLESS BABY HORROR

POLICE
TEC
CHAK
CHAK

Second night out and already breaking into the Gotham City P.D..Good to see you're right back on track, Selina...
Let's hope you're not too out of practice, because it would be really embarrassing to get caught here.
anodyne
PART TWO OF FOUR
ED BRUBAKER-WRITER
DARWYN COOKE-ARTIST
MIKE ALLRED-INKER
SEAN KONOT-LETTERER
MATT HOLLINGSWORTH-COLORIST
MATT IDELSON-EDITOR
NACHIE CASTRO-ASST. EDITOR

Looks like they've beefed up the security since my last visit...

CHANK

Not that they'll stop me, but it does make it more complicated.
POOM!

WHAT THE HELL--?!
FIRE!
DEEOOO

DEEOOO DEEOO

OO DE

SKANG
SKANG

POP!

WHAT'S ON FIRE?!
FWOOSH
FWOOSH
I DON'T KNOW!

SERGEANT, WE'VE GOT A PROBLEM HERE...

NEGATIVE ON THAT FIRE, BUT WE'VE GOT A POSSIBLE SECURITY BREACH.

FULL PERIMETER CHECK-- NOW! ANY INTRUDER SHOULD BE CONSIDERED ARMED AND DANGEROUS!

I'VE GOT NOTHING ON THE SECURITY CAMS, SIR...
NO, NO... OF COURSE YOU DON'T. DAMN IT.
B2
RECORDS & MORGUE

CALL IN-- ANYONE GOT ANYTHING?
MORGUE

NEGATIVE.
I GOT NOTHIN'!

ALL CLEAR UP HERE.
ALL RIGHT, KEEP LOOKING, DAMN IT. SOMETHING'S GOING ON...
CHIK

They're probably searching the whole complex by now, but it should be safe down here.

SNIK

Not like there's anything of real value in the morgue...

But it does have what I'm looking for--

Information.
Jane Doe 4

RREEEEEEEE

Jane Doe #2
Jane Doe #3
Jane Doe #4

TEC

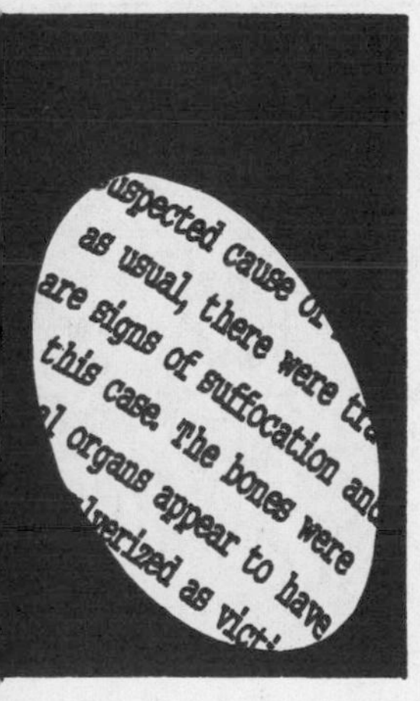
suspected cause of
as usual, there were
are signs of suffocation
this case. The bones were
organs appear to have
as

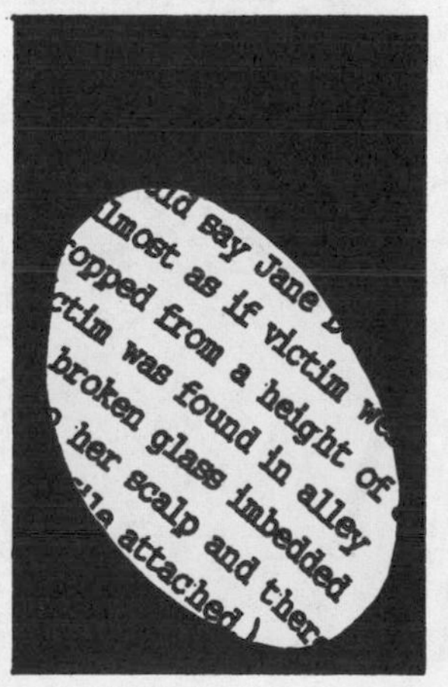
say Jane
almost as if victim
dropped from a height of
victim was found in alley
broken glass imbedded
her scalp and
attached.)

Damn it--
It's just
like Holly
said...

IT'S BEEN GOING ON FOR WEEKS, SELINA...
... BODIES ARE JUST TURNING UP IN ALLEYS, ALL BEATEN AND BLOODY.

MOST OF THE GIRLS I KNOW ARE SCARED TO DEATH.
ARE THE POLICE PUTTING ANY MORE MANPOWER ON THE STREETS?

HA! RIGHT. THEY COULDN'T CARE LESS! YOU KNOW HOW IT IS... WE'RE NOT REAL CITIZENS TO THEM.

YEAH...

... I GUESS I DO KNOW HOW THAT IS.

NICE TO SEE THAT NO MATTER HOW MUCH GOTHAM CHANGES, SOME THINGS STILL STAY THE SAME...
... LIKE HOW MOST OF THIS CITY WOULD LOVE FOR THE WHOLE EAST END TO JUST FALL INTO THE ATLANTIC.

SO, YOU WANT TO TELL ME WHY YOU LEFT THE *CONVENT?* AND WHY YOU'RE BACK WORKING ON THE *STREETS?*
OH, *C'MON,* SELINA. IT'S NOT LIKE *THAT...* IT'S JUST...

... THAT PLACE WASN'T *RIGHT* FOR ME, OKAY? I COULDN'T *HANDLE* IT.
AND I SURE AS HELL WASN'T GONNA BECOME A *NUN!*

IT WAS GOOD ENOUGH FOR *MAGGIE.*
NO... IT *WASN'T.*
MAGGIE LEFT *WITH ME.*

WHAT?! WHEN DID *THIS* HAPPEN?

A *LONG* TIME AGO, SELINA... WE WENT OUT TO THE WEST COAST. BUT I LOST TRACK OF HER A COUPLE OF YEARS AGO AFTER SHE FELL IN LOVE WITH SOME GUY...
... THEN I DRIFTED BACK TO GOTHAM LAST YEAR.

I DON'T *GET IT...* I THOUGHT MAGGIE'D FOUND HER PEACE IN LIFE?
I THINK SHE HAD A *CRISIS OF FAITH,* SELINA... IT HAPPENS.

WHY DIDN'T EITHER OF YOU TRY TO *CONTACT* ME?
I *KNOW.* BELIEVE ME... I JUST THOUGHT... *DAMN...*

FOR THE LAST FEW YEARS, WE THOUGHT YOU WERE *DEAD.*
Umm... WELL...

Oh... YEAH.

WELL, YOU CAN'T BELIEVE EVERYTHING YOU READ.

NO, APPARENTLY *NOT*.
SO, WHAT HAPPENS NOW, SELINA?

NOW?

WELL, *FIRST* WE'RE *BOTH* GOING TO GET SOME MUCH NEEDED *SLEEP*...

... AND THEN *TONIGHT*...

... I'M GOING TO GO OUT AND TRY TO STEAL US SOME *ANSWERS*.

Guess they won't mind if I borrow their copier...

I'd rather not just take this report, on the off-chance the cops decide to get off their butts and actually do something.
B2
RECORDS & MORGUE

WHIIRRR-CHK-WHIIIRR-

WHIIRRR-CHK-WHIIRRR-CHK-

OR
WHIIRRR-CHK-

WHIIRRR-CHK-WHIIIRR-
HELLO?
IS SOMEONE THERE?

WHIIRRR-CHK-WHIIIRR-CHK-WHIIIRRR

WHIRR-CHK-BEEP

WHAT THE HELL IS *THIS?*

WHAM
CLASSIFIED INFORMATION, I'M AFRAID.

This really isn't a good start to your new life, Selina...
THUMP!

Making amateur mistakes and assaulting cops.

So, where do I go from here?
Solving crimes hasn't exactly been what I'm famous for.
But still, with all my experience on the other side of the law...

... Maybe I can see things that the police would never notice.
ROYAL
EEERRRK

Sometimes a different point of view is enough.
ROYAL

But that isn't the real problem.

The real problem is the police aren't looking that hard for clues in the first place.

For the exact reason Holly said...

These murder victims don't qualify as people to them.

And as long as the killer isn't bragging to the media, their deaths are acceptable.

Their pain is the price of doing business.

Like paying taxes.

So who speaks for them, then?
If not the police?

Batman?

No. While he may care, these women aren't that high on his list, either.

As far as he's concerned, they've chosen a life of crime, and while victims, they are far from innocent.

But I've felt the fear they feel, and the pain.

The pain of that lost innocence.

And once you've lost that, it's so much easier for them to just take everything else, too.

So... who speaks for them, then?
el GATO
CHEWING GUM
... OH, GOD... NO... PLEASE...

... MAKE IT STOP...
SOMEONE PLEASE...

WHY IS THIS HAPPENING TO ME?

... WHAT DID I DO?

... PLEASE...

HEY... IS, uh...
IS EVERYTHING
OKAY?

WHAT?!

AW, GAWD!
NOOO!

AAAHAASHH
HELP!

SOMEBODY HELP!
HELP ME!
WAIT!
STOP!

SOMEBODY HELP ME!
YOU DON'T UNDERSTAND...

CHEWING GUM
CALL 911!

el GATO
CHEWING GUM

SOMEBODY HELP!

SPANG

ROWRR!

Damn.

Too late.

WHAT THE HELL IS GOING ON...?

Does this guy somehow think he'll be less conspicuous running down the street naked instead of in blood-stained clothes?

Oh, I see...

So much for running down the street. But that still doesn't explain him stripping.
Maybe that's just his thing...

In any case, let's see what he left behind...

No money, no I.D.... Just this...
DAVE'S ALL NITER

WHHEEEEEOOOOOOOO
Damn.

OVER HERE!
WHEEOOO
BAR
WHHEEEEEOOOOOOO

NO...
NO, I *DIDN'T* GET A GOOD LOOK.
HIS FACE WAS ALL COVERED IN *BLOOD.* I COULD ONLY SEE HIS *EYES,* PEERIN' *OUT* AT ME...
... THOSE EYES...

OKAY, BURTON... I NEED YOU TO CORDON OFF THIS AREA.
AND FISCHER--

FISCHER?! WHAT THE *HELL* DO YOU THINK YOU'RE *DOING?*
Aw, *C'MON,* SARGE...
SHE'S *JUST* A HOOER...

YEAH, I KNOW. AND *PROTOCOL* SAYS THE OFFICER IN *CHARGE* ROLLS THE STIFF.

NOW *GIMME* THAT, YOU STUPID ROOKIE!

ROTTEN PIGS...
FREEZE!

They walk in her blood to take her last ten dollars, because they think she's not a person. But they're wrong...
She was. They all were...
WHO *SAID* THAT?!
And I will speak for them. Because no one else will.
el GATO

DOCTOR THOMPKINS,
I THINK I NEED
MORE ANASETTIC...

NO, IT'S GOING TO BE ALL RIGHT... JUST RELAX.

Dr. Les

AM I GONNA DIE, DOCTOR THOMPKINS?
OF COURSE NOT...

TAP

'CAUSE I DON'T FEEL SO GOOD... I THINK I SHOT MYSELF...

DANNY SAID IT WASN'T LOADED, THOUGH...

TAP
TAP
TAP
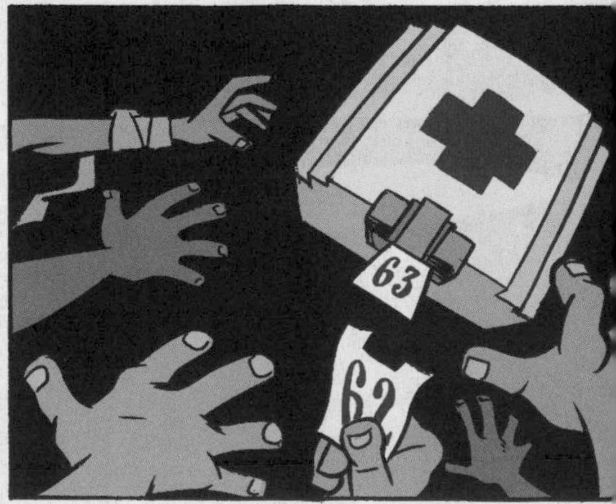
63
62

TAP
TAP
TAP

WHAT *IS* THAT TAPPING?
TAP
TAP
TAP
TAP

58
26

IT FEELS LIKE I'M FLOATING...

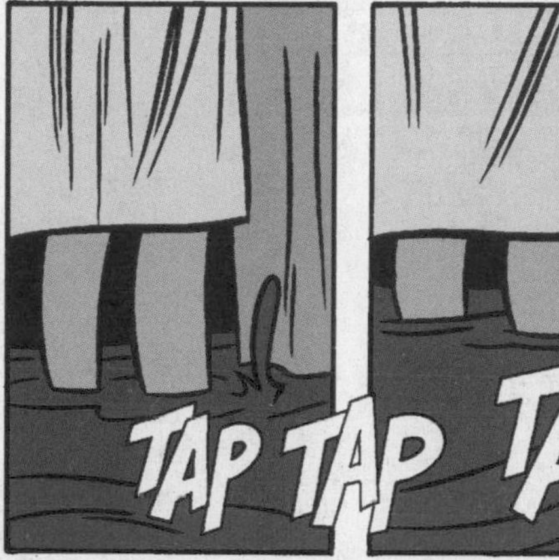
TAP TAP TAP

TAP

TAP
TAP

TAP
TAP
TAP

WHU --?

OH, GOD... JUST A DREAM...

TAP
TAP

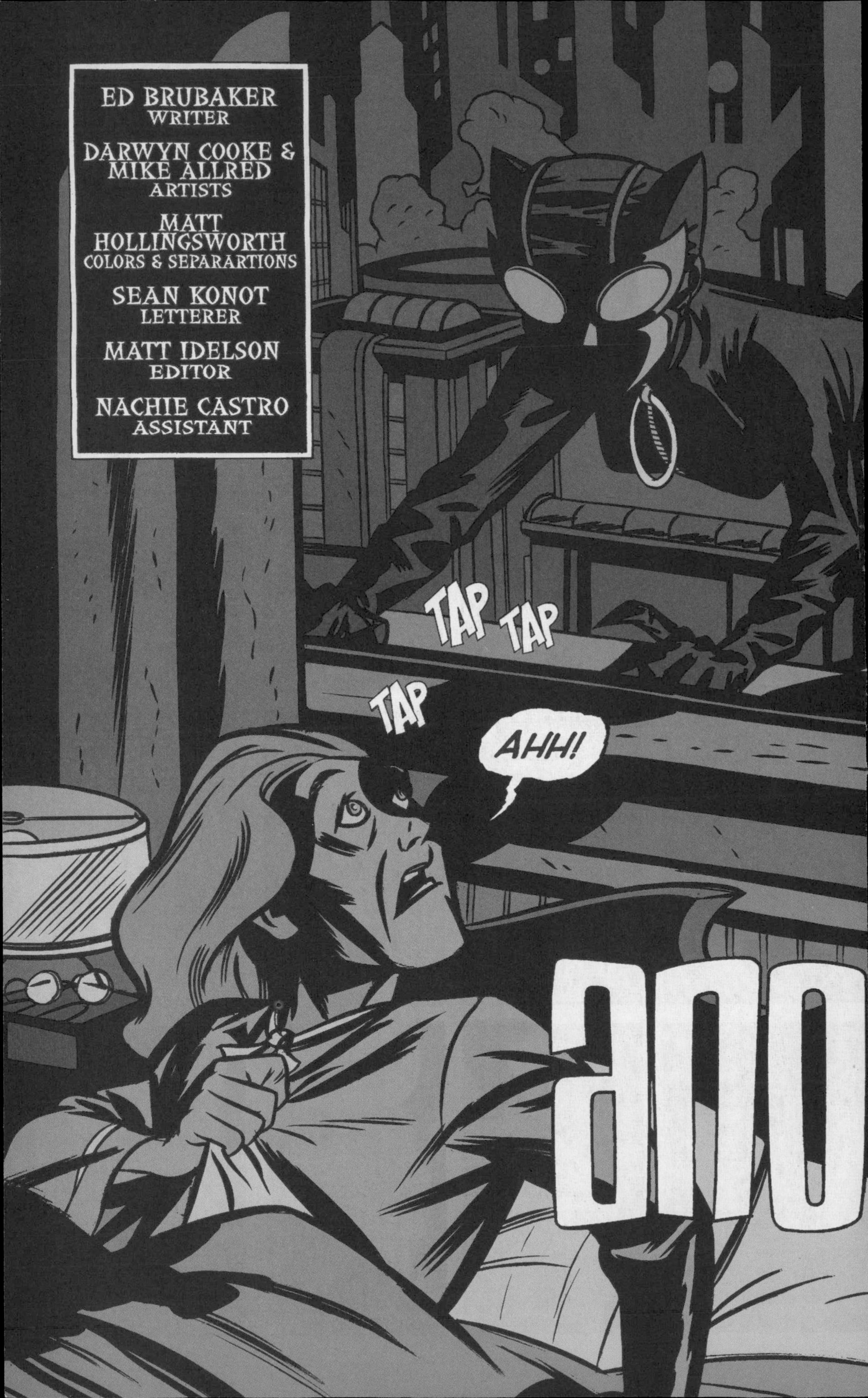

ED BRUBAKER
WRITER
DARWYN COOKE &
MIKE ALLRED
ARTISTS
MATT HOLLINGSWORTH
COLORS & SEPARARTIONS
SEAN KONOT
LETTERER
MATT IDELSON
EDITOR
NACHIE CASTRO
ASSISTANT
TAP TAP
TAP
AHH!

part 3
dyne
LESLIE? I'M REALLY SORRY TO BOTHER YOU SO EARLY...
SELINA?
WHAT ARE YOU DOING OUT THERE? YOU NEARLY SCARED THE LIFE OUT'VE ME...
YEAH, SORRY ABOUT THAT, BUT I DIDN'T KNOW WHERE ELSE TO GO...
WHAT IS IT? YOU'RE NOT IN TROUBLE, ARE YOU?
NOT FOR THE MOMENT, NO. I'M TRYING TO HELP SOLVE SOME TROUBLE, ACTUALLY...
YOU'VE PROBABLY HEARD ABOUT THESE RECENT PROSTITUTION MURDERS?

Uh, YES... I HAVE.

HOW CAN I HELP?

WELL, THERE'S SOME-ONE THE BATMAN USES WHEN HE NEEDS INFORMATION...

A WOMAN CALLED ORACLE...
BUT I DON'T EXACTLY HAVE HER PHONE NUMBER...

... AND I NEED SOME INFORMATION, FAST.
I HAVE THAT NUMBER, SELINA.

I COULD CALL FOR YOU, IF THAT'S WHAT YOU'RE ASKING.

IF SHE KNOWS IT'S FOR ME, SHE MAY NOT WANT TO--

I'LL MAKE HER UNDERSTAND, DON'T WORRY.

I NEED WHATEVER SHE CAN GET ABOUT THIS CAR, I WROTE DOWN THE LICENSE AND MAKE AND MODEL.

THANK YOU, REALLY...

I'LL CALL YOU AS SOON AS I HAVE ANYTHING.

I'M SORRY I HAD TO WAKE YOU UP.
IT'S ALL RIGHT... I APPRECIATE THAT YOU KNOCKED INSTEAD OF JUST BREAKING IN.

I LIKE THE NEW LOOK, BY THE WAY... IS IT HELPING YOUR SLEEP ANY?

MORE THAN I CAN EVEN SAY... REALLY...

And it's true... The last few nights, since I've been going out like this...
... I've been sleeping like a baby.
I haven't felt this good since the first few months I was wearing the mask.
And maybe it has as much to do with having some idea of a mission, as it does with the mask.

THE EAST END...
HOW MUCH LONGER'RE YOU GUYS GONNA BE? IT'S AFTER FOUR A.M....
WE'LL BE DONE WHEN WE'RE DONE, OFFICER... THIS IS A CRIME SCENE INVESTIGATION, NOT A TRACK MEET.
WHAT THE HELL...?
GATO
CHEWING GUM

MAYBE IF YOU BOYS IN BLUE'D DO A LITTLE LESS WALKING ALL OVER POTENTIAL EVIDENCE, WE COULD GET OUT OF HERE A BIT SOONER...
YEAH, WHATEVER...
HEY, JERRY... COME LOOK AT THIS.

WHATTAYA GOT?
I'M NOT SURE IT'S ANYTHING, BUT IT'S WEIRD...
...TAKE YOUR TIME.

YEAH, WEIRD... BUT MAYBE THIS MUD WAS SOFT EARLIER OR SOMETHING.
OR IT WAS A REALLY FAT CAT.

NAH, IT HASN'T RAINED IN WEEKS, AND THIS IS HARD PACKED...
...SEE? I HARDLY MADE A DENT.
WHAK

OKAY, SO MAYBE IT WAS A REALLY REALLY FAT CAT. IT'S WEIRD, I AGREE, BUT I DON'T THINK IT PERTAINS TO THIS INVESTIGATION, CHRIS...
... I'M AFRAID THE ONLY EVIDENCE WE'RE GONNA FIND THAT'S USEFUL IS THE LICENSE PLATE ON HIS CAR. AT LEAST WE CAN TRACK THAT DOWN.

UNLESS YOU THINK THESE HOOKERS ARE ALL GETTING KILLED BY A CAT?
KLIK

Um,
SELINA...?

THERE'S, Uh...
SOMEONE'S ON THE
PHONE FOR YOU.

THEY HAVE
A *NAME?*

LESLIE
SOMEONE...
I *FORGET,*
THOMPSON?

ROWR!

LESLIE, HI... NO, IT'S FINE...
SHE DID, HUH? YEAH, LET ME GET A PEN...

OKAY, I'M READY... YEAH...
YEAH... WELL, I DON'T KNOW IF THAT'S GOOD OR BAD...

NO, I'M GOING TO LOOK INTO IT, DON'T WORRY...
NO, THANK YOU, LESLIE...

BEEP!

SELINA... AREN'T YOU EVEN GONNA TELL ME WHAT THAT WAS ABOUT?
NOT RIGHT THIS SECOND... I'M GOING TO SLEEP FOR ANOTHER HOUR...
BUT DON'T MAKE ANY PLANS FOR THE AFTERNOON...

... THERE'S A JOB I NEED YOU TO DO.

Honest Jay Little
USED CARS
EXCUSE ME, MA'AM...
9000

IS THERE ANYTHING SPECIFIC YOU'RE LOOKING FOR?
BECAUSE YOU SEEM LIKE THE KIND OF WOMAN WHO'D FIT PERFECTLY BEHIND THE WHEEL OF THAT CLASSIC PORSCHE CONVERTIBLE YOU'RE LOOKING AT.

I WAS THINKING THE SAME THING, REALLY... ARE YOU HONEST JAY LITTLE?
THAT'S ME, JUST LIKE ON THE SIGN... WHY DO YOU ASK?

WELL, I FIGURED IF YOU WERE THE OWNER, WE MIGHT BE ABLE TO GO SOME PLACE PRIVATE TO... NEGOTIATE THE PRICE.
IT'S A LITTLE OUT OF MY RANGE.

A-- A BUSINESSMAN IS ALWAYS WILLING TO NEGOTIATE... JUST COME INTO MY OFFICE AND WE CAN GET MORE COMFORTABLE.
THAT'S JUST WHAT I HAD IN MIND.
OFFICE

Hunh-- GUESS I LEFT MY BLINDS CLOSED...
JUST ONE LESS THING TO WORRY ABOUT THOUGH, RIGHT, HONEY?

HEY, WHAT THE HELL IS GOING ON?!

SLAM!
IS THIS A SETUP?!

SOMETHING LIKE THAT...
... EXCEPT WE'RE NOT AFTER YOUR MONEY.
AAAHH!!!

OOMMPH!

THREE AND A HALF WEEKS AGO YOU SOLD A '72 DODGE SEDAN TO A MURDERER. DO YOU KNOW WHAT CAR I'M TALKING ABOUT?

YEAH, I KNOW... THE COPS WERE RAKIN' ME OVER THE COALS ABOUT IT TODAY 'CAUSE I DIDN'T CHECK ENOUGH PAPER ON THE BUYER...
WHAT'S IT TO YOU?

I'M ASKING THE QUESTIONS, HONEST JAY...

WHO WAS THE BUYER?
I DON'T KNOW-- HE JUST HAD A CHECK CASHING I.D., BUT IT DIDN'T REALLY LOOK LIKE HIM.

WHAT DID HE LOOK LIKE, THEN?
SERIOUSLY? HE LOOKED A HELLUVA LOT LIKE TODD RUSSELL, THE ACTOR.
I KID YOU NOT...

I DIDN'T TELL THE COPS THAT, THOUGH-- OR ABOUT HIS I.D. BEIN' FAKE.
ARE YOU TRYING TO TELL ME A FAMOUS ACTOR IS MURDERING THESE WOMEN?

NAW. IT WASN'T HIM... HE JUST LOOKED LIKE HIM. THE VOICE WAS ALL WRONG.
SO... uh... YOU'RE NOT GONNA BLOW THE WHISTLE TO THE HEAT, ARE YOU? I'M JUST TRYIN' TO MAKE A LIVING, Y'KNOW?

I GOT A WIFE AND KIDS.

I'M NOT INTERESTED IN HOW YOU CHEAT THE I.R.S., HONEST JAY...
BUT YOUR LACK OF RESPECT FOR YOUR WIFE...

NOW, THAT'S A DIFFERENT STORY ALTOGETHER.

MOVIE NEWS WEEKLY

OKAY-- I NEED YOU TO GET OUT THERE AND TELL EVERYONE YOU KNOW NOT TO TAKE ANY DATES WITH GUYS WHO LOOK LIKE MOVIE STARS...

WHAT'RE YOU GOING TO DO?

WELL, I'VE GOT *ONE* MORE LEAD TO CHASE DOWN TONIGHT, BUT IT MEANS A LITTLE UNDERCOVER WORK...
DO YOU-- DO YOU THINK WE REALLY SHOULD'VE JUST *LEFT HIM* LIKE THAT?

OH, C'MON HOLLY-- DON'T TELL ME YOU'VE *COMPLETELY* LOST YOUR SENSE OF *HUMOR.*

NO, I JUST DON'T WANT TO GET ANYONE IN ANY *TROUBLE,* THAT'S ALL...

YOU KNOW AS WELL AS I DO, THERE'S *NO AVOIDING* TROUBLE...
MOVIE NEWS WEEKLY
INSIDE THE LIFE OF TODD RUSSELL

Which is what I'm telling myself around nine that night as I nurse a drink in the diviest bar in the East End...
... dangling myself as bait for a killer.
Which is possibly not the brightest idea I've ever had.
DAVE'S
ALL NIGHTER

THIS SEAT TAKEN?
HELP YOURSELF.

SO, uh... I HAVEN'T SEEN YOU IN HERE BEFORE, HAVE I?
I DON'T KNOW, MAYBE.

OH, WELL... I'VE GOT THIS *PLACE* NEAR HERE, IT'S KIND OF AN OLD FACTORY BUILDING, BUT I'VE GOT A LITTLE *APARTMENT* IN IT... SORT OF...
I JUST THOUGHT, MAYBE IF YOU WERE TRYING TO FIND A *PARTY*...
AND...?
WHAT KIND OF PARTY IS *THAT?* JUST THE *TWO* OF US?

I DON'T KNOW, FROM WHERE *I'M* SITTING, IT LOOKS LIKE IT'D BE A PRETTY *GREAT* PARTY THAT WAY.
MY-- AREN'T WE *FORWARD?*

I'M SORRY, MAYBE I GOT THE WRONG IDEA... ARE YOU WAITING FOR SOMEONE?
KIND OF...
A GUY WHO LOOKS A LITTLE LIKE TODD RUSSELL. I MET HIM IN HERE ONCE...

HUNH-- DOESN'T SOUND FAMILIAR...

WOULD YOU EXCUSE ME FOR A MINUTE, I NEED TO USE THE HEAD...

Great, Selina... maybe if you're lucky you'll be batting off flies all night.
BIGANTE

Good to know my disguise is working, I guess, and at least that guy was sort of cute. Now if my movie star look-alike would just show up.
BIGANTE

That's some long bathroom break, guess I scared him...

WAIT A SECOND...
BIGANTE

BIGANTE

HEY! THAT'S THE MEN'S--!
MEN

CRACK!

Damn it...

DAMN IT.

Of course, it's Gotham, so of course he's got to be a freak...

Damn it.
HEY, ARE YOU OKAY?
MEN

YOU OKAY...?
YOU WANT A BEER OR ANYTHING?
NAH, I'M GOOD...

IT'S BEEN A CRAZY NIGHT SO FAR ANYWAY, SO I PROBABLY SHOULDN'T DRINK.

TELL ME ABOUT IT...
... BEFORE I MET YOU I ALMOST PICKED UP AN UNDERCOVER COP.
FFFTTT

"REALLY? HOW'D YOU FIGURE IT OUT?"
"SOMETHING SHE SAID, I GUESS...
"JUST FELT WRONG SUDDENLY. INSTINCT."

SO, YOU LIKE, LIVE HERE?
YEAH-- THE RENT'S CHEAP...
HA HA HA!

Damn it. I had him right in front of me and I was too blind to see it.

ACTUALLY, MY FAMILY OWNS THIS BUILDING.SO I USE THIS AS AN APARTMENT WHEN I'M IN THE CITY...

What did he say? He lives in an old factory building...?
There are at least a few of those in the East End.

Y'KNOW... I USUALLY DON'T GO TO PLACES, LIKE APARTMENTS AND STUFF, WITH NEW GUYS...

"... IT'S JUST NOT SAFE THESE DAYS."

BUT YOU SEEM LIKE SUCH A NICE GUY, TODD...
I LIKE TO THINK SO...

I MEAN, YOU TOTALLY DON'T SEEM LIKE THE KIND OF GUY WHO'D HURT A GIRL.

WHAT'S WRONG, BABY?
Uh... NOTHING...

I JUST HAVE TO USE THE HEAD...

OH GOD... OH GOD... DON'T LET IT HAPPEN AGAIN...

Come on, Selina, move... It's been nearly an hour. He probably has someone there already...
Wherever there is... Still two more abandoned factories to check.
That is, if he wasn't just lying to me...

But no matter what, if another girl dies tonight, I'm going to feel responsible...

... IT'S OKAY... IT'S GONNA BE JUST FINE... JUST MAINTAIN CONTROL.

DAMN IT... PLEASE... DON'T DO THIS...

HEY, *TODD?*
IS EVERY-THING, um... *ALL RIGHT?*

YOU'VE BEEN IN HERE A *WHILE* AND--

EEEIIIAA!!!

WAIT! IT'S NOT WHAT YOU *THINK!*

EEEIIIAA!!!

WAIT!

WAIT! LET ME EXPLAIN!

WHOMP!
--OOOFF!

ALL RIGHT, SO EXPLAIN...
... I'M ALL EARS.

Sometimes you just get lucky... Not usually, but sometimes.

Of course, I've always thought I had better luck than most people, certainly...
... But tonight, on the trail of a killer...
By the skin of my teeth...

NINE
EEIIAAA!
... I literally arrived in the nick of time.

And if that's not luck, I don't know what is.

anodyne

CONCLUSION

ED BRUBAKER
WRITER

DARWYN COOKE &
MIKE "DOC" ALLRED
ARTISTS

MATT HOLLINGSWORTH
COLORS & SEPARATIONS

SEAN KONOT
LETTERER

MATT IDELSON
EDITOR

NACHIE CASTRO
ASSISTANT

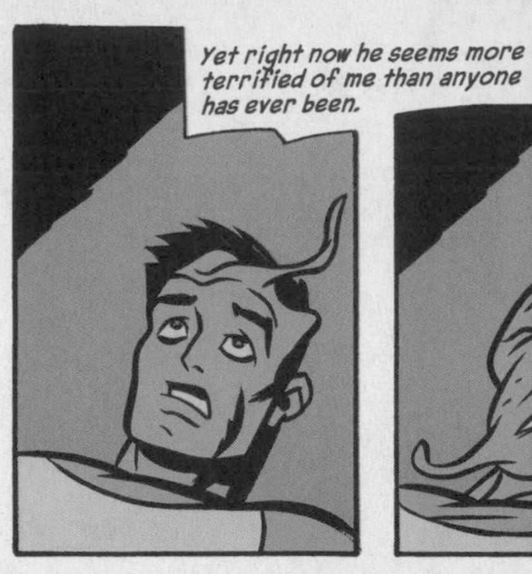
Yet right now he seems more terrified of me than anyone has ever been.

... YOU DON'T UNDERSTAND...

I SWEAR...

Something about this just isn't right...

MAYBE YOU'D BETTER EXPLAIN THIS ALL TO ME, AFTER ALL...
NOT JUST NOW, NO.
WHAT? YOU-- YOU'RE NOT GONNA HURT ME...?

YOU WERE THERE THE OTHER NIGHT-- IN THE ALLEY...
I HAD TO CHANGE TO GET AWAY...
BARELY MADE IT...

CHANGE?

MY GOD... THE CAT.
CHEWING GUM

"I WAS JUST ON THE STREET ONE DAY, AND THAT'S THE FIRST THING I CAN REMEMBER CLEARLY...

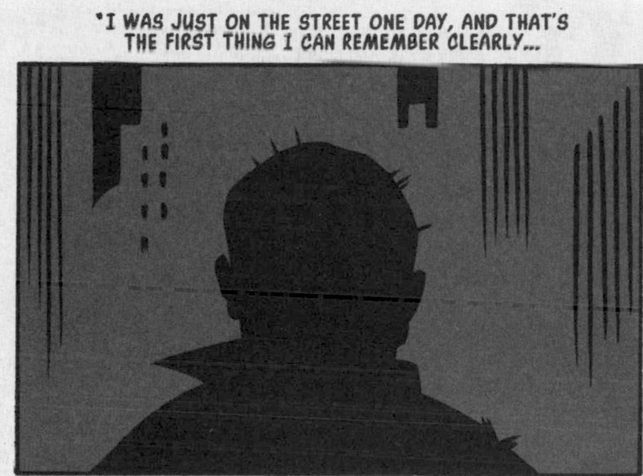

"MY FACE DIDN'T LOOK RIGHT... I WASN'T SUPPOSED TO BE UGLY...

"SO I FIXED IT."

YOU COULD JUST DO THAT? HOW DID YOU KNOW?
I DIDN'T KNOW... I JUST WISHED IT, I GUESS...

WHAT ABOUT BEFORE THAT DAY, DO YOU REMEMBER ANYTHING AT ALL BEFORE THEN?
JUST LITTLE FLASHES...

"A WAR OR SOMETHING...

"... THEN, I DON'T KNOW...
"PEOPLE LOOKING AT ME, ALL THE TIME.
"HURTING ME.
"I REMEMBER MY HAND... GROWING BACK...
"THEN NOTHING... JUST A LOT OF LITTLE PIECES, BUT NOTHING THAT MAKES SENSE...

"... UNTIL THAT DAY... JUST SUDDENLY *BEING THERE*. AND EVERYONE LOOKING AT ME."

BUT I NEVER WANTED TO HURT ANYONE... I SWEAR...
... I JUST HAD TO STOP THEM FROM SEEING WHAT I WAS...

... IT'S LIKE A NIGHTMARE...

IT'S GOING TO BE OKAY... I THINK I KNOW SOMEONE WHO CAN HELP YOU.
YOU-- WHAT?

I'M AFRAID YOU'RE JUST GOING TO HAVE TO TRUST ME ON THIS ONE, THOUGH...
BUT... I...

YOU'RE JUST GOING TO HAVE TO TRUST ME, SERGEANT... THIS WON'T DO YOU ANY HARM.

NO!
YOU'RE TAKING ME BACK TO THEM!

WAIT. WHAT'RE YOU--
YOU'RE A LIAR!

LIAR!
Well, that went well, Selina... Let's not forget the whole "psycho" aspect of our psycho killer.

STAND STILL!

STOP RUNNING, DAMN YOU!

SKLURCH!

Oh, yeah... That was effective...

NO!

UNNHH!
SKASH

NO MORE RUNNING!

NO MORE ANYTHING!

WHOMP!

Don't know if this'll work...

SNIK

... But I have to try something.

CHU
NO!

NOT SO INVULNERABLE AFTER *ALL*, HUH?
SKLORP!

DON'T GET YOUR HOPES UP...

JUST A *MINOR* SETBACK, REALLY.

Oh my god...
I can't beat him.

Have to
get away.
I have to get away.
This is too big for me...

I SAID, NO MORE
RUNNING!

No!

Damn it!
CRASH!

YOU
REALLY
SHOULDN'T'VE
LIED TO
ME...

Oh...

The hell
with it...

ZZZZZT!

GZZAAP

THAT... HURT...
... BUT YOU *STILL* DON'T GET IT, DO YOU?

OH...

I WOULDN'T SAY *THAT*...

SKLASH!

WHAT'VE YOU DONE?
Y'KNOW, I'M NOT REALLY SURE...

OH, GROSS.
SPLORCH

WAIT, WHAT'RE YOU DOING?

DON'T--

WAIT!

I really hope this works...
SLAM

KLMPT!

GLORP!

SKLOOOOSH
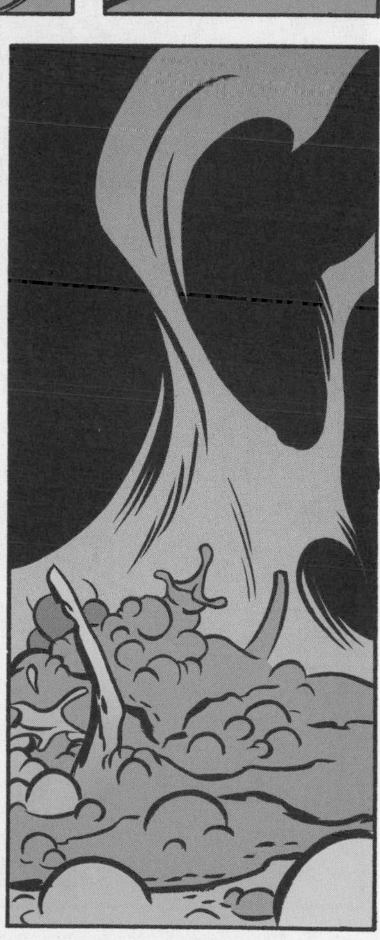

GNAAA!

I don't think I'm going to be able to move if that thing gets up again... Please don't let it get up...
Okay, Selina, what now? What are you going to do with the head in that freezer?
Oh, I know... He'll know what to do with it. He's used to things like this. I'll just have to figure out how to find him...
But maybe I'll just lie here for a while first...

I DON'T CARE, SELINA...

... YOU'RE NOT TO USE THE SIGNAL AGAIN, UNDERSTAND? THAT'S FOR THE POLICE.

I DIDN'T KNOW HOW ELSE TO GET HOLD OF YOU. YOU SHOULD REALLY GET A BEEPER OR SOMETHING...
I DON'T THINK SO.

IN HERE?
YEAH, BUT... uh... BE CAREFUL.

CHANK!

PLEASE... HELP ME...

... HELP ME...

SO THEN WHAT HAPPENED, SELINA?
I DON'T KNOW... I GUESS HE TOOK IT WHEREVER HE TAKES THINGS LIKE THAT.
ARKHAM ASYLUM OR S.T.A.R. LABS. SOMEPLACE.
NATIONAL

MAN, I CAN'T BELIEVE IT... YOU USED THE SIGNAL. THAT IS SO COOL.

YEAH, IT WAS KIND OF COOL...
SO ANYWAY, I'VE BEEN THINKING, HOLLY...

... I'M NOT SURE EXACTLY WHERE I'M GOING WITH THIS WHOLE HELPING PEOPLE THING... BUT ONE THING I DO KNOW...

... I DON'T WANT YOU OR ANYONE ELSE I CARE ABOUT WORKING ON THE STREET.

SO, I WANT TO HIRE YOU.

HIRE ME? TO DO WHAT?

WELL, IF I'M GOING TO TRY TO DO THIS RIGHT, I NEED SOMEONE WHO BLENDS IN WITH THE STREET LIFE A LITTLE BETTER THAN I DO ANYMORE...
... SO, I WANT YOU TO BE MY EYES AND EARS.

IT'S A HIGH-PAYING GIG, BY THE WAY.
I'VE STASHED AWAY A LOT OVER THE YEARS, ENOUGH TO LIVE ON COMFORTABLY FOR THE REST OF OUR LIVES. AND IF THAT RUNS OUT...

... WELL, I CAN ALWAYS GET MORE, CAN'T I?

SO... WHAT DO YOU SAY?
I SAY, WHEN DO I START?
YOU ALREADY DID... IT WAS YOU WHO BROUGHT THESE MURDERS TO MY ATTENTION IN THE FIRST PLACE...

SO JUST KEEP DOING WHAT YOU DID.
OKAY, SO THEN, WHAT DO WE DO NOW?

WELL, TONIGHT I'LL BE GOING OUT AGAIN, BUT RIGHT NOW I'VE GOT TO GO SEE A FRIEND...
... SOMEONE I OWE A LOT TO.

SELINA, I CAN'T ACCEPT THIS...
LESLIE, I INSIST... IT'S JUST TO HELP YOU RUN THINGS A LITTLE.
IT'S REALLY NOT MUCH, YOU DESERVE A LOT MORE.

IT'S JUST-- WELL...
I PROMISE YOU, THE PEOPLE WHO LOST IT DESERVED A LOT WORSE... AND I'M SURE THEY NEVER MISSED IT, EITHER.
OH, VERY WELL... BUT YOU REALLY DON'T HAVE TO DO THIS. I GET QUITE A FEW GRANTS TO RUN THIS PLACE, REALLY.

I KNOW, BUT I JUST WANT TO GIVE SOMETHING BACK TO YOU. WHETHER YOU MEANT TO OR NOT, YOU HELPED ME THROUGH A HARD TIME, HELPED ME FIND MY FEET...

... AT LEAST I THINK YOU DID.
YOU KNOW, HE TOLD ME... ABOUT WHAT YOU DID...

... THAT MAN KILLED ALL THOSE WOMEN, AND YOU STILL TRIED TO HELP HIM. IT'S AMAZING.
YEAH, WELL... YOU'D HAVE DONE THE SAME THING. AND REALLY, HE WASN'T COMPLETELY RESPONSIBLE...

SO... HOW DOES IT FEEL, SELINA KYLE? TO HELP AND NOT JUST TAKE?
I'M NOT SURE... GOOD, I GUESS... BUT STRANGE...

WHAT DO YOU MEAN?
IT'S HARD TO SAY... KIND OF OVERWHELMING, I GUESS. LIKE I'M WORRIED THAT I'LL FAIL.

AND I'M NOT USED TO FEELING THAT WAY.
CLINIC
I AM...

... DON'T WORRY, SELINA, YOU'LL DO JUST FINE.

And you know what? I think maybe she's right. Because for a long time all I could think about was pain-- my own and my family's. And that pain defined who I was, and ultimately just caused more...
Until there was nothing left for me beyond that.

But today I'm not thinking about the crooked Cops and politicians. I'm not thinking about the wife-beaters and rapists, the mobsters...
SMILE
I'll get to them all, eventually.

No, right now, all I can think about is how good I'm going to feel when that sun goes down...

And you can't argue with happiness, can you?
End

BATMAN

THE QUEST FOR JUSTICE CONTINUES IN THESE BOOKS FROM DC:

FOR READERS OF ALL AGES

THE BATMAN ADVENTURES
K. Puckett/T. Templeton/
R. Burchett/various

BATMAN BEYOND
Hilary Bader/Rick Burchett/
various

BATMAN: THE DARK KNIGHT ADVENTURES
Kelley Puckett/Mike Parobeck/
Rick Burchett

BATMAN: WAR ON CRIME
Paul Dini/Alex Ross

GRAPHIC NOVELS

BATMAN: ARKHAM ASYLUM
Suggested for mature readers
Grant Morrison/Dave McKean

BATMAN: BLOODSTORM
Doug Moench/Kelley Jones/
John Beatty

BATMAN: THE CHALICE
Chuck Dixon/John Van Fleet

BATMAN: CRIMSON MIST
Doug Moench/Kelley Jones/
John Beatty

BATMAN/DRACULA: RED RAIN
Doug Moench/Kelley Jones/
Malcolm Jones III

BATMAN: FORTUNATE SON
Gerard Jones/Gene Ha

BATMAN: HARVEST BREED
George Pratt

BATMAN: THE KILLING JOKE
Suggested for mature readers
Alan Moore/Brian Bolland/
John Higgins

BATMAN: NIGHT CRIES
Archie Goodwin/Scott Hampton

BATMAN: NINE LIVES
Dean Motter/Michael Lark

BATMAN: SON OF THE DEMON
Mike Barr/Jerry Bingham

CATWOMAN: SELINA'S BIG SCORE
Darwyn Cooke

COLLECTIONS

BATMAN: A DEATH IN THE FAMILY
Jim Starlin/Jim Aparo/
Mike DeCarlo

BATMAN: A LONELY PLACE OF DYING
Marv Wolfman/George Pérez/
various

BATMAN BLACK AND WHITE Vols. 1 & 2
Various writers and artists

BATMAN: BRUCE WAYNE — MURDERER?
Various writers and artists

BATMAN: BRUCE WAYNE — FUGITIVE Vol. 1
Various writers and artists

BATMAN: BRUCE WAYNE — FUGITIVE Vol. 2
Various writers and artists

BATMAN: CATACLYSM
Various writers and artists

BATMAN: CHILD OF DREAMS
Kia Asamiya

BATMAN: DANGEROUS DAMES & DEMONS
Dini/Timm/various

BATMAN: THE DARK KNIGHT RETURNS
Frank Miller/Klaus Janson/
Lynn Varley

BATMAN: THE DARK KNIGHT STRIKES AGAIN
Frank Miller/Lynn Varley

BATMAN: DARK KNIGHT DYNASTY
M. Barr/S. Hampton/G. Frank/
S. McDaniels/various

BATMAN: DARK VICTORY
Jeph Loeb/Tim Sale

BATMAN: EVOLUTION
Rucka/Martinbrough/Mitchell/
various

BATMAN: GOTHIC
Grant Morrison/Klaus Janson

BATMAN: HAUNTED KNIGHT
Jeph Loeb/Tim Sale

BATMAN/HUNTRESS: CRY FOR BLOOD
Rucka/Burchett/T. Beatty

BATMAN IN THE FIFTIES
BATMAN IN THE SIXTIES
BATMAN IN THE SEVENTIES
Various writers and artists

THE KNIGHTFALL Trilogy
BATMAN: KNIGHTFALL Part 1: Broken Bat
BATMAN: KNIGHTFALL Part 2: Who Rules the Night
BATMAN: KNIGHTFALL Part 3: KnightsEnd
Various writers and artists

BATMAN: THE LONG HALLOWEEN
Jeph Loeb/Tim Sale

BATMAN: NO MAN'S LAND Vols. 1 - 5
Various writers and artists

BATMAN: OFFICER DOWN
Various writers and artists

BATMAN: PRODIGAL
Various writers and artists

BATMAN: STRANGE APPARITIONS
S. Englehart/M. Rogers/
T. Austin/various

BATMAN: SWORD OF AZRAEL
Dennis O'Neil/Joe Quesada/
Kevin Nowlan

BATMAN: TALES OF THE DEMON
Dennis O'Neil/Neal Adams/
various

BATMAN: VENOM
Dennis O'Neil/Trevor Von Eeden/
various

BATMAN VS. PREDATOR: THE COLLECTED EDITION
Dave Gibbons/Andy Kubert/
Adam Kubert

BATMAN: YEAR ONE
Frank Miller/David Mazzucchelli

BATMAN: YEAR TWO — FEAR THE REAPER
Barr/Davis/McFarlane/various

BATGIRL: A KNIGHT ALONE
Puckett/D. Scott/Turnbull/
Campanella/various

BATGIRL: SILENT RUNNING
Puckett/Peterson/D. Scott/
Campanella

BIRDS OF PREY
Various writers and artists

BIRDS OF PREY: OLD FRIENDS, NEW ENEMIES
Dixon/Land/Geraci/various

CATWOMAN: THE DARK END OF THE STREET
Brubaker/Cooke/Allred

THE GREATEST BATMAN STORIES EVER TOLD Vol. 1
Various writers and artists

THE GREATEST JOKER STORIES EVER TOLD
Various writers and artists

NIGHTWING: A KNIGHT IN BLÜDHAVEN
Dixon/McDaniel/Story

NIGHTWING: ROUGH JUSTICE
Dixon/McDaniel/Story

NIGHTWING: LOVE AND BULLETS
Dixon/McDaniel/Story

NIGHTWING: A DARKER SHADE OF JUSTICE
Dixon/McDaniel/Story

NIGHTWING: THE HUNT FOR ORACLE
Dixon/Land/Guice/Zircher/various

ROBIN: FLYING SOLO
Dixon/Grummett/P. Jimenez/
various

ROBIN: YEAR ONE
Dixon/S. Beatty/Pulido/
Martin/Campanella

ARCHIVE EDITIONS

BATMAN ARCHIVES Vol. 1
(DETECTIVE COMICS 27-50)
BATMAN ARCHIVES Vol. 2
(DETECTIVE COMICS 51-70)
BATMAN ARCHIVES Vol. 3
(DETECTIVE COMICS 71-86)
BATMAN ARCHIVES Vol. 4
(DETECTIVE COMICS 87-102)
BATMAN ARCHIVES Vol. 5
(DETECTIVE COMICS 103-119)
All by B. Kane/B. Finger/D. Sprang/
various

BATMAN: THE DARK KNIGHT ARCHIVES Vol. 1
(BATMAN 1-4)
BATMAN: THE DARK KNIGHT ARCHIVES Vol. 2
(BATMAN 5-8)
BATMAN: THE DARK KNIGHT ARCHIVES Vol. 3
(BATMAN 9-12)
All by Bob Kane/Bill Finger/various

BATMAN: THE DYNAMIC DUO ARCHIVES Vol. 1
(BATMAN 164-167,
DETECTIVE COMICS 327-333)
B. Kane/Giella/Finger/Broome/
Fox/various

WORLD'S FINEST COMICS ARCHIVES Vol. 1
(SUPERMAN 76,
WORLD'S FINEST 71-85)
B. Finger/E. Hamilton/C. Swan/
Sprang/various

**TO FIND MORE COLLECTED EDITIONS AND MONTHLY COMIC BOOKS FROM DC COMICS,
CALL 1-888-COMIC BOOK FOR THE NEAREST COMICS SHOP OR GO TO YOUR LOCAL BOOK STORE.**

Visit us at www.dccomics.com

BM0012